Butterflies In The Breeze!

Nature poems for children.

Shreeja Narayanan

BookLeaf
Publishing

India | USA | UK

Dedication

To my father, late Dr. P.K. Narayanan,

Who taught me the power of words and the beauty of

expression...

To Sree,

The one who stands by my side through every challenge

and triumph...

To my wonderful son,

Who fills my heart with love...

To every child who has ever touched a flower,

Listened to the birds sing,

Or danced in the rain.

May you always find your heart in the rhythms of

nature.

Preface

Butterflies In The Breeze , is a collection of poems that celebrates nature through the eyes of a child. It also has a couple of nature folk tales from around the world. The poems in this collection were written keeping the curiosity and joy of childhood in mind.

As a child, I often found myself fascinated by simple elements and things in nature —a tiny ladybug crawling over a green leaf, cloud shapes in the blue sky, or a burst of colors blooming in the garden. These poems are an invitation to slow down and notice the world around us in all its glory. Some poems might make you giggle, while others might spark a moment of quiet reflection.

To the children who read these poems, I hope they spark a sense of adventure and a lifelong love for the natural world. And to the grown-ups who may read these poems aloud, I hope you rediscover the magic of nature through the eyes of a child. Let the adventure begin, with every page you turn.

Acknowledgements

I am deeply grateful to those who have supported me in bringing this collection of poems to life. Each poem is a reflection of the beauty, wonder, and lessons nature offers us, and I owe my ability to capture these moments to all of you!

1. The Blue Sky Mimes With Signs

The blue sky mimes with signs,
Visual tales divine!
Look up and you shall see,
sombre knights on a hunting spree!
fluffy rabbits with bouncy tails,
and mighty ships with milky sails.

The **Cumulus** fools the mind's eye,
when you look up and sigh,
at the spongy cotton balls
and fleecy sheep with white overalls.
Then I see a great white steed,
running across the vast, misty mead.

It is the **Cirrus** then,
that floats high up when,
the morning weather is cold
and thin wisps of silvery cobwebs unfold.
"Brrrrrr!" you say.

In bed you stay.

The **Nimbus** roars, "Beware!"
There's no time to spare.
Dark grey skies, lightning streaks,
Bellowing thunder, overflowing creeks,
Heavy rains,
Verdant terrains!

Wait a little, spare a second.
Stop a little and reckon,
the visual tales divine as
the blue sky mimes with signs!

2. Nature's Palette

Aquamarine gems
On Cerulean jars ,
Turquoise butterflies
Perching on stars.

Crimson garnets
On a Czar's crown,
Carmine poppies
Bordering the town.

Spring green Parrots
Screeching on a tree,
Jades and Emeralds
Glittering with glee.

Tangerine butterflies
On a lemony daffodil,
Fluttering merrily
Over brooks tranquil.

Pink marshmallows
All nice and chewy,
Fuchsia orchids
Brilliant and dewy.

Mauve roses on
Lavender robes,
Aubergine vineyards
And Wisterian groves.

A speckle of blue and a spot of red,
A streak of yellow and a stipple of pink.
A dash of green to calm the soul
With a trace of mauve to halt and think.

A myriad of hues and a slew of shades
Bewitch the eyes and entice the mind.
With nature's palette of colors galore,
Paint a picture and unwind!

3. The Secret Of The Fireflies

Tiny dots of fiery light,
soaring high after dark,
like bright little speckles,
With a sprightly spark!

Dancing in numerous circles,
shaping radiant arcs,
like miniscule, beaming fairies,
and rejoicing meadowlarks !

like little silver moonbeams
peeping through grey clouds,
like miniature twinkling stars
shimmering among crowds !

like teeny, luminescent blooms at night,
swaying on the forest floor,
like glowing plankton on the moonlit sea
floating towards the shore!

To be a beacon of light and hope,
is the secret the fireflies hold,
close to their hearts
And with wonder, we behold...

4. The Ocean's Lullaby

The Ocean sings lullabies,
for the ones who listen.
The Ocean plays lilting tunes,
for forlorn eyes that glisten.

Its frothy waves ebb and flow,
sometimes fast and sometimes slow.
Sometimes they whisper,
sometimes they roar.

The ocean sings with the breeze.
The Ocean hums at ease.
A hushed gush with a soothing whistle,
like the gentle murmur of swaying thistle.

The ocean's offspring answer
from deep within,
The dolphins whistle,
The whales sing.

On a soulful moonlit night,
when the ocean is a mirror,
one can hear its silent lullaby,
melodious and clear.

For a lost soul seeking company,
For a restless wayfarer pursuing peace,
The Ocean sings lullabies,
The Ocean warbles with the breeze!

5. The Caterpillar Song

I'm a cuddly caterpillar
with feet sixteen,
all slender and wobbly,
squeaky and clean!

I'm a mighty eater,
with a big, green head
and eight pairs of shiny boots
all of them red!

I'm a master of disguise,
I sport colors bright,
I mimic twigs and leaves
and stay out of sight!

I am a silk spinner,
I weave and spool,
my cocoon so smooth
and soft like wool!

And then I doze off,
one fine day.
It's probably 'M*etamorphosis*'
I hear them say!

I've been waiting for this, my entire life,
to turn into a fluttering petal so light,
so exquisite, so vibrant,
Oh! Such a winged delight!

6. Grampa's Mango Tree

Tall and proud,
The mighty mango tree
stands in *Grampa's* backyard,
for all to see!

With a majestic trunk
and gnarled roots,
with emerald green leaves
and golden yellow fruits!

Robins whistle
and nightingales sing.
They perch on the crown
as dawn sets in.

Tiny red ants in a row,
unanimously they clamber!
To savor the luscious fruit
that's sunshine and amber!

Down slide furry squirrels
with the dappling sunshine,
playing 'Hide n Seek'
on a morning so divine!

"I want a treehouse,"
said the little boy!
But *Grampa* made a lovely swing
for him to enjoy!

The wind pushes the swing so high,
It almost breaks free,
The mighty mango tree looks on
as the little boy claps with glee!

Now *Grampa* smiles down from the heavens
and the little boy has grown,
but in the backyard still stands the mango tree
proudly for all to see!

7. The Woods Can Cast A Spell

Shhh! The woods have magic!
They can cast a spell,
Now If you silently listen,
you can surely tell!

When the towering trees whisper,
it's time to know.
The timeless spell has begun,
a subtle breeze begins to blow!

The Oaks and the Maples
share a knowing glance,
The Autumn leaves whisper,
The sunbeams dapple and dance.

Beneath the verdant canopies,
the twisted vines swing!
Rabbits scramble and squirrels hide,
To their mother's bosom, the tiny owlets cling!

A miracle unfolds in the moist air,
In hushed tones, as the Capuchins chatter,
The silver brook begins to babble,
The singing larks fly and scatter!

Its time for the mysterious fog,
to conceal and hover
as the queer, old spell
finally takes over!

Now there is wonder
and there is peace,
I can discern the woodland dwellers,
I can converse with the silent trees!

The enchanting spell has worked!
Immensely have I healed!
The woods know this!
The secret is revealed!

So the woods weave magic!
They can cast a spell!
They can heal and connect,
They can make you get well!

8. The Dance of The Winged Wonders!

Vibrant petals, Oh! so light!
Flutter away in the sunlight!
Sit on flowers, so very bright
and suck nectar with delight!

Red, rotund pearls,
with black, round spots!
A ladybug so pretty,
proudly she trots!

A tiny, little hummingbird,
tiny as tiny can be,
flapping and hovering,
for all to happily see!

A majestic dragonfly
with prismatic eyes,
and translucent wings
that take to the skies!

A busy, little worker bee
scurrying for its queen,
With yellow stripes on black
a uniform with majestic sheen!

Nature's darlings with lovely wings,
dance gleefully, for a few springs,
These winged wonders are joyful things
Tiny warriors and tiny kings!

9. A Glimmer In The Glade

A tranquil glade
stands proudly in the woods,
near the duck pond,
where a mighty Beech once stood!

The glade looks boundless,
in the midst of towering trees,
You can spot the stars
and sway with the dancing breeze!

The glade is idyllic,
home to birds galore!
It sings a soothing lullaby
that leaves you wanting more!

The glade is a riot of colors,
as seasons come and go!
With petunias, pansies, poppies and peonies,
it puts up a brilliant show!

The glade lets you rest
and time stands still,
Then you see a sunlit path
that goes up a verdant hill!

As I leave the glade,
to walk up the path,
I see a glimmer
that grows into a swath!

The glimmer in the glade
in your spirit, stokes a fire,
It's a glimmer of hope,
that tells you to follow your heart's desire!

10. The End Of The Rainbow

Tiny pearls of raindrops
and the bright sun shine,
give rise to a vibrant rainbow,
So prismatic! so divine!

Seven colors, seven segments
look like seven smooth slides!
They beckon you to enjoy
thrilling roller coaster rides!

"What's at the end, though?"
I have always wondered!
"It's a pot of Gold," they say,
that the leprechauns plundered!

The treasure remains hidden
under one color they said...
Is it violet, indigo, blue or green?
Or Maybe yellow, orange or red!

As you glide along,
one slide at a time,
Shimmery fairies wave
and distant bells chime.

Great white unicorns
with their silky tails,
And fluffy cloud ships
with their milky sails!

As you glide along yellow,
you see a treasure so old.
Beneath dazzling vines,
you see the pot of Gold!

It is healing radiance
that fills the sacred pot!
and to get this secret treasure
you must give it a shot!

More beautiful is the journey
than the journey's end,
Enjoy the vibrant rainbow slides
and not just the golden send.

11. Blossoms So Bright!

Fiery bursts of orange red,
crown a flaming Gulmohur,
towering tall, above your head!
Delicate petals, dancing flares,
symbolize warmth,
as one stares.

Blossoms, purple and pale pink,
adorn the majestic Magnolia,
standing gracefully by the ice rink!
Fragrant petals, so light and pure,
symbolize femininity,
Oh! How they allure!

Glossy leaves with blooms milky white,
embellish the Frangipani,
much to a poet's delight!
Scented petals, surreal and divine,
symbolize spirituality.
May their guiding light shine!

A symphony of colors, nature unfolds,
with brilliant blossoms and brilliant blooms,
a rare secret, each one holds!
like kisses of the Earth,
arise the blissful flowers,
from nature's cozy hearth.

12. The Stallion and The Unicorn

Out in the wild ,
at the speed of light,
glides a jet black stallion
like a falcon in flight!

With pride in its heart
for all to see,
It's a symbol of power
wild and free!

So untamed, yet so gentle!
Intuition as its guide,
conquering treacherous terrain
with every stride!

The unicorn is no less,
a monarch of the endless sky,
and a peaceful angel
that soars so high!

Ethereal and full of hope,
ivory and white,
a symbol of purity
healing and bright!

Galloping through the midnight mist,
a magical being with a unique horn!
Among all things rare and precious
is the elusive unicorn !

A powerful redeemer, a formidable force,
A healing guardian, a celestial source!
Sail through life like a stallion so rare
Heal and charm like a unicorn with flair!

13. The Rain Symphony

Sleek Streaks of silver lightning
whizz past charcoal clouds,
Distant claps of thunder Boom
and Crackle out loud!

What an inky black night!
Thru the rustling leaves,
the lone wind Whooshes
The spider silently weaves!

Little Joe looks out
as the raindrops drip,
'Pitter Patter' on the window pane
Frogs Croak while beetles flip!

Playful Rover barks
as fireflies twirl,
in an arc, around a lamppost,
dancing with a swirl.

The Earth heaves a sigh
with the symphony of the rain!
As the night goes by,
dawn shines upon the plain!

The raindrops hum a lilting lullaby,
Sing along the robin and the thrush
with dulcet tones and soft trills
flute like whistles and a crooning hush!

The symphony plays on, echoing and clear,
in the distant peaks, so misty and gray,
The day winds up in the wink of an eye
humming a tune as the sky fades away.

14. Christmas Magic

Out in the winter wonderland
beyond holly trees and frosty snow,
sets the distant sun,
with a pink, golden glow!

Trotting reindeers and naughty elves,
With sparkling eyes so wide,
peep at snowmen with carrot noses
gliding along snowy slides!

By the fireplace, so warm and cozy,
hangs my stocking, red
waiting for gifts galore,
and the 'Swoosh' of Santa's sled!

Jingle bells and fairy lights
adorn the Christmas tree,
Silver balls and candy cane
with a tree topper star to see!

Hot Chocolate, so creamy and rich,
gingerbread cookies and plum cake,
roast turkey with cranberry sauce
and all that mother can bake!

Christmas Carols, we ring in,
Friends, Cousins and I,
with melody and rhythm in our voice
and a twinkle in the eye!

Christmas ropes in joy,
Christmas brings in cheer,
Christmas reels in kindness
as it welcomes the New Year!

15. The Animal Parade!

Furry brown squirrels
scamper on boughs,
look in nooks and crannies deep
for treats to eat and nuts to keep!

Beneath a mighty tree,
moos a fat, white cow
swishing its dusty tail,
winking at a snoopy quail!

A nosy, little pup and a tiny, grey kitten
chase a big, black, bumble bee!
Not one to give up, the haughty bee
drives the two up a tall tree!

Deep in the green grass,
slithers a slender, slimy snake .
It wriggles left and it wriggles right
looking for prey day and night!

A handsome red rooster
with a vibrant feather fan,
digs for wriggly grub
near the dense, bushy shrub!

Pesky green parrots up a mango tree,
with monkeys as their friends,
they fetch from passersby
and mimic them on the sly!

The animal parade is fun to watch,
they speak a common tongue
that is often loud and clear
only if you wait to hear!

16. A Day By The Sea

The pristine coast, so pure and white
with coconut trees standing upright!
Turquoise waves ebb and flow
hit the shore, quick and slow!

Snails and sea shells, ivory and bright,
on the grainy sand, grey and light!
Tiny, floating ships, so distant and faint
dot the horizon, like speckles of paint!

Seagulls grey in the clear, blue sky
screech, squawk, caw and cry!
till they snatch some slimy fish
from the sailor's feeding dish!

On the sea shore, children play
with sand castles, pebbles and some clay,
with wiggling toes and grainy hands,
thru the waves, they sift the sands!

Dusk sets in, the sun takes a dip
The humpbacks sing and dolphins flip!
The sky turns pink and merges with the sea,
The day has ended for you and for me!

17. An Echo in the Mountains

Behind the babbling brook
and the whispering pines,
stand mountains majestic
so tall and so divine!

Grey and brown with a dollop of snow,
boulders and rocks down below
Towering over vales with a cave or two,
Misty waterfalls flowing through!

I stand at the edge,
and shout out loud
There goes my voice
and bounces off the clouds!

The rocky cliffs play with me,
a game of 'Peek a Boo'!
They toss back an echo
that sounds like me too!

The echo in the mountains
is so clear yet so low!
just like friendly banter
of old friends from long ago!

18. The Diver and The Deep Sea

The deep sea calls
the diver so brave,
to traverse its great depths
and its watery grave!

What lies below is a secret,
The diver knows it though!
Echoes of the past
far away down below!

Treasure chests and sunken ships,
Relics in copper Gold,
Forgotten cities in a row,
Fossils of warriors old.

Anemones and Sea urchins
play with Anglers and Eels
Coral reefs so vibrant
and Barnacles on Seals!

Hammerheads and Humpbacks
on a racing spree ,
Dolphins leap and Manatees glide
in their world, vast and free!

The ocean beckons the diver
with so many mysteries!
The diver with no fear,
sees endless possibilities.

An Oyster with a Pearl,
so lustrous and so rare!
The sea rewards the diver
for he knows how to dare!

19. The Windmill On The Hill

Near the green woods
over the verdant hill,
stands a lone windmill
so proud and still!

The wind glides along,
The blades take a chance
They swirl and dance
as the wind gives a glance!

The farmer sits inside
as the mill stones grind
barley, wheat and dry fruit rind,
into flour so refined!

A baker rotund and a kind, old *Gran*
need some flour to bake
Cranberry pies and fruit plum cake
and cheese crackers to make!

The windmill stands near a brook,
come hail, wind, rain or snow!
As people come and go
The flour here is the best they know.

The wind mill needs the playful wind,
it cannot spin on its own!
or twirl its blades and the mill stone.
or grind flour alone!

The wind does a little dance.
The wind mill twirls with speed,
A friend in need,
is a good friend indeed!

20. The Tale of Maui and the Sun

Maui, the warrior brave,
Loved his people so dear,
A demigod, with powers great,
he changed their very fate!

The sun was a trickster,
haughty and bright!
It often raced away
leaving people in dismay!

"We need more sun!"
the people cried.
"More time to sow!"
"More time to plough!"

Mighty Maui fought fierce winds
and climbed the hills so steep,
He lay in wait for the mighty sun
as it came to sleep.

Maui lassoed the sun around
with a rope of fierce, white light!
The brilliant sun fought back
with all its very might!

Maui was strong, he tamed the sun!
"Slow down Sun!" he barked with rage.
The sun obliged, with a sigh,
and slowed its course across the blue sky!

And so the people had a lot of time
to sow, to plough and to live in peace!
They revered Maui, their God of might,
who saved the day and gave them light!

21. The Formidable Five!

Fiery flames so fierce and bright,
warms the cold and gives us light!
Sometimes, it does rage and roar,
wrecking life and burning more!
'*Agni*' as she is known
can be a good friend or a foe alone!

The whistling wind is a gift so rare
a gentle breeze, a breath of air,
sometimes it can howl and blow
thru homes and hearths and raze them low.
'*Vayu*' the wind, is a secret untold,
a blessing or a curse, from eons old.

The Earth so solid, sturdy and deep,
The ground we walk and the bed we sleep.
Earth, when troubled, shakes and cracks,
to cause landslides, quakes and attacks.
'*Prithvi*' as we fondly call,
is the only home left, for one and for all.

Water so pure, it gives us life,
quenches thirst, ends our strife.
But when it rages, wild and free,
It floods the land, disrupts the sea.
'*Jal*' is a blessing day and night,
A gift of wellness, when the time is right!

Space, the vast and endless sky,
stretches wide, so far and high.
holds the air, the light and the sound,
A quiet place where peace is found.
'*Akash*' the heaven, so ethereal, so vast
embraces the present, future and past!